Third edition published simultaneously in 1997
by Exley Publications in Great Britain and
Exley Giftbooks in the USA.
Second edition published in Great Britain in 1990 by
Exley Publications.
Second edition published in the USA in 1992 by
Exley Giftbooks.
First edition published in Great Britain by Exley
Publications in 1976, revised and updated in 1990
Copyright © Exley Publications, 1976, 1990, 1997
ISBN 1-85015-845-2

Front cover illustration by Richard de Cesare
Back cover illustration by Laura Brydon, age 7
Above illustration by Richard Wakeford, age 7

Typeset by Delta, Watford, Herts.
Printed and bound in the UAE.

**Exley Publications Ltd, 16 Chalk Hill, Watford,
Herts WD1 4BN, United Kingdom.
Exley Giftbooks, 232 Madison Avenue,
Suite 1206, NY 10016, USA.**

To Lincoln and Dalton

Other books in the series
Happy Birthday!
(you poor old wreck)
Grandmas and Grandpas
(you lovable old things)
**To Mum (UK),
To Mom (US)**
(the kindest of ladies)

■ EXLEY

NEW YORK · WATFORD, UK

To Dad
(you poor old wreck)

Dads have a pretty fundamental place in the hearts of their children. Kids may poke fun at Dad, but the love remains strong, and it shows even in the funniest entries. Dads are fun to be with, and love being laughed at and laughed with.

TO DAD was originally created in the 1970s, from entries sent in from schools all over the world – Britain, the United States, Australia, New Zealand, Jamaica, Denmark, Germany, Spain, Holland and many other countries. Now, this ever-popular book has been updated for the 1990s. Much, of course, remains the same. Dads remain pre-occupied with work, whether it's driving a truck, milking the cows or dashing off to a new world of computers. And their traits show a remarkable consistency – from their love of cars to their oft-alleged laziness around the house.

But, however busy they are, however pre-occupied with work, money, and supporting their kids, dads still find time for play, for a lesson in life, for a tickle.

You'll find lots of grammatical errors and spelling mistakes in the book. We have felt it right to leave the entries just as we received them. So no prizes for finding "printer's errors"! All the entries, together with their often very creative illustrations, are the genuine work of the children.

We hope you'll have as much fun reading the book as we've had editing it. If the book comes to you as a gift from your own child, we're sure he or she would endorse many of the things that are said. And we'll be surprised if some of the passages don't bring a lump to your throat. For the love kids have for Dad comes across loud and clear.

Richard & Helen Exley

What is a dad?

Fathers like to think they are responsible, dutiful, orderly and enthusiastic and they endeavour to convince their children of this.

Julia *Age 1.*

A father's shoulder is something to sit on when there is a crowd and you can't see.

Jacqueline Small

Hayley *Age*

When my dad comes in from work the house fills with laughter

Thomas Telford *Age 1*

Antony Masters Age 5

All shapes and sizes

Dads wear socks so that We can not see there hairre legs.

Sara Beesley

My dad often wears a yukky green sweater with holes in the elbows. He says that these holes are there so that his elbows can breathe.

Rebecca Skett *Age 11*

Victoria

Dad has got a sweet tooth,
And I mean a sweet *tooth*
He's had all the rest pulled out!

Lisa *Age 10*

Karen Murray *Age 10*

My father likes comfortable clothes, like old corduroys and flannel shirts, they look a bit messy though, so we have to dress him up in respectable clothes.

Emma *Age 10*

I like my daddy's
poggy tummy
I like to feel it squige.
I like my mummy's
poggy tummy
but its not as good
as his.
Bryony

My dad is a bit bald,
My dad is fat,
My dad isn't old
Well not quite yet.

Jane *Age 11*

Paul Lowe *Age 7*

Only a father would ride on the roller coaster with me, come off with a green face and say he had a good time.

Loni Casale *Age 11*

Fathers are sometimes thin on top and some are as bold as babies rear end

Dave Clark *Age 14*

A father is a man mother but unlike a mother he is not always on the telephone.

Clare Dawkins

In the crazy world of television, people seem to think that dads are funny things that live in paint-pots and jump up and down on the best dining-room table singing about Birdseye puddings. In fact they are not. They are really perfectly sane things that would spank you if you tried to do the same.

Guy Hannaford

Thomas *Age 8*

Dad and the TV

A dad is someone who watches TV while he's sleeping.

Myrna Knutson *Age 8*

My dad watches TV when it isn't on.

Valerie Caplan

When my father comes home at night. After dinner he sits down and watches football, football, football. If you were to say the house was on fire while he was watching TV he would say "Thats nice".

Guy Zuckermann *Age 12*

Daddies are for yelling at you to leave the football game on the television.

Mothers are for yelling at your daddy to shut up and change the channel.

Rhoda Sampson *Age 13*

Brett Hanson

A Father is someone
to watch
tv with

When my mommy
goes out
my dad has to go to
his mommy
and have dinner!
Jason Age 9

My dad is
strong.
He's alvay
He hamma
his fum
he did.

Theodore Thomas

Poor old Dad. . .

**My dad tries to play golf,
Trys to ski,
Trys to play tennis
But so far he just hasn't
been lucky.**

Philip *Age 12*

Dad gets your french homework wrong.
Dad sleeps in his armchair all Sunday.
Dad is someone who trys to explain how the
kitchen shelf fell down.
Dad fixes the car and then has to send it to the
mechanic to be repaired.
Dad had to walk five miles to school when he was
a boy.
Dad was almost picked for the Olympics.

David

ip to things he is.
is fum, Once he hammed
e had to go to hospital

Karen *Age 8*

Father

Somebody that I
Can come to when
I'm sick
Worried
Wrong
Somebody that
Can tell me the
Solution
To life
AND
Progress;
And give me
HOPE
To go on.

Helen Holm *Age 10*

Ali Abbas Hanif *Age 8*

In praise of dads

My father is someone who makes me feel like Pete Sampras if I get a service in.

Scott Strong *Age 11*

What I like best about my dad is that he is proud of me when I do well in class, and even when I do badly he is still proud of me. I love him for that.

Anjanee Bissessarsingh *Age 10*

If I didn't have Pa I think the world would be grim. He always help me with mi multiplications.

Darrell James

Dads love you more than anyone

Claire Powell *Age 9*

Thank heavens for dads

They are very busy people but they are never too busy to give you a kiss.

Katharine Rule *Age*

Thank heavens someone invented dads.

C. Matthew

A dad is a comferter. He comforts my mother when she can't reach her dreams. He cares fer us when she is upset or even mad.

Margaret *Age*

My father is very funny and very pleasant. When he comes back home from work and is very tired, he cheers up as soon as he sees us.

Nadia Caraccio *Age*

I want the whole world to know my dad is very nice and kind to me.

Sharon Chapler *Age*

When I don't go to school in the afternoon and my father is free from work, we talk a lot. Even when he is very tired he is ready to listen to my problems and he always knows how to advise me.

Barbara Frasca *Age 1*

Mark Farrell

Life's truths

Who let me help him fix a broken car?
Who showed me love when I grew up?
Who told me the honest way to go?
Who smoothed the slippery way for me?
This tribute goes to my father.

Michelle Ellery *Age 13*

My dad has taught me to think, before I go to bed, over what progress I've made during the day. He always encourages us to read more books, increase our knowledge and vocabulary and enrich our language. His special motto is "Service before self" and he has taught me: "First deserve and then desire."

Arnitabh R. Shah

Meropi Hambi *Age 5*

"Pull your socks up,
 make your bed,
Tuck your shirt in,
 get a haircut,
Clean up your room,
 brush the dog,
Fix your tie,
 brush your teeth,
Take those jeans off,
 they're filthy,
What did you say
 to me then?"

Andrew *Age*

Simon Perrin *Age*

The boss

My dad thinks his the boss. So do I.
It's not Fair my dad gets the biggest dinner and
dessert my dad likes it.
My dad Throws his smelly soucks at me.

Michelle *Age 10*

A dad is a person that thinks he knows
everything but doesn't even understand simple
new math.

Melissa Wellington *Age 10*

Fathers all like listening to the family radio, and
most of them like reading.
If their wife wants to read they usually get
impatint, but if they want to read their wife isn't
allowed to be impatint.

Margaret *Age 10*

When anything goes wrong, Dad is completely unbiased and blames me.

Michael Haworth-Maden *Age 12*

Lazybones

A dad is someone who says he will do something some time, but the time never comes.

John

My dad has a funny hobby which I think is being lazy.

James Age 8

Dads are never working unless they are forced to by mothers.

David Age 12

My dad believes in everybody doing their fair share. So that when we go into the living room after cutting the grass, we see him lying on the sofa and watching T.V.

Julie Age 11

Bruno Orsini Age 13

A dad is someone who will finish making a cupboard in the year 3000!

Joyce Blair

My dad is brilliant but lazy too because he always stays in bed when I am up. When he is not watching I sit on his tummy and start thumping him but he says it does not hurt him.

Amber Macdonald *Age 10*

ome typical dad's talk:
'll fix the door tomorrow."
But the hardware store's shut."
"But the ladder is broken."

Genevieve

The breadwinner

A dad is One of the most Important people in a family because he helps mom to earn money to keep the whole family living. So that means that a father is some-one who Cares for you. A father is a thing that you depend on.

Simon M. Leese

A dad is a person who puts a roof over your head. And who gives you a nice warm bed.

And puts food on the table for you to eat. And pu` shoes on you little bare feet.

Guy Miller Age 8

Lisa Ann Millett Age 1 ?

Don't know what he does, but in the evening, when he gets home his face is tired. Sometimes he comes home at lunch, and the talk is full of his meetings with strange people about strange things. The need for money, and those who suffer from the government. Land being taken over, or rents not paid.

This happens for the full week, but in the week-end he is different. Same bright eyes in a bright face, his black hair shining in the sun.

Douglas *Age 12*

Fathers are for earning money, so mothers can spend it.
Pam Munroe *Age 11*

Despite his office work, he is one who will always be with you.

Douglas *Age 12*

Arielle Griffiths *Age 8*

BOB

Life without dads

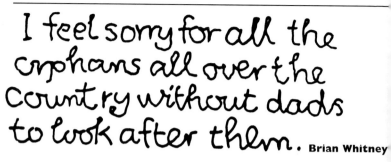

I feel sorry for all the orphans all over the country without dads to look after them. **Brian Whitney**

I don't know what I would do without my dad I would not have any Cristmas presents No birthday presents No food no shelter No were to live No nothing.

John Seane *Age 9*

We're lucky to have a dad. With no dad we would have no food, no home. If people had no children the world would have no people, no heroes, no heroines.

Ryan

Sarah Galant

A very
A very
is what
should

Caroline Greenwood Age 8

happy mother
happy father
happy family
e like

Tracy Hampton *Age 6*

Dad is away

My mother goes quietly up to bed,
I start to think of the tears she might shed.
Dad has gone and we're alone,
To live in this house of cold stone.
And he won't be back for another six months.

... Dad is coming home tomorrow,
Now there will be no more sorrow.
It's nice to see mommy happy again,
I can see a tremendous change.
It's great having him home.

Angela *Age 15*

Big, strong and kind

Fathers are big and strong and kind.

Aine Hunt *Age 1*

Dad helps me through my doubts and fears.

Ruth James *Age 1*

A father is someone who when he comes home from work and is tired still listens to you talking. A father is someone who understands you.

Lois Looering *Age 1*

Dads are the ones who when it's Mother's Day buys a present and says its from you.

A. McAuilhin

James *Age 6*

I always feel safe with Dad.

Anne Fowka *Age 11*

A father is
the backbone
of a family.
Paul Marshall *Age 12*

Katy Low

In the home a dad is very important. He is the person who helps to provide us with money to fee and clothe ourselves. He can paint your bedroom, fix your radio, makes cages for your pets, repair a puncture in your bicycle and help you wit your history homework. A dad can be very useful for taking you in the car to and from parties, music lessons, and dancing lessons. A dad is the person whom you ask for extra money. He is the one who complains about the time you spend talking on the telephone, as he has to help mom pay the bills. A dad is someone who will support you in an argument if he believes you to be right. He is someone who hears about your school results, and treats you if they are good. A dad likes to come into a nice happy home in the evening, and settle back in his chair with a newspap

Beverley Wilkins *Age 1*

Dads are for giving you money, being boss, gardening, and any other pleasures that they can think of; that includes sleeping under a newspape and pretending to be reading it.

Deborah *Age 1*

Although dads do not show it, they worry abou you an awful lot.

Beverley Wilkins *Age 13*

What are dads for?

Dads are helpful
and in every way,
They are not only there
to do your hair
But to undo
sticky problems.
That's why Dads
are there.

Sarah Edworthy Age 11

Fathers are for erning money
and helping to keep the human
race going.

Susan Abbott Age 10

Peter Fey Age 10

Being with Dad

Now dad, he is the nice guy,
He'll sit and watch TV
And sheer bliss are the evenings
When I'm sitting on his knee.

Susan Harvie *Age 10*

As a small child, I will always remember our family sitting beside a roaring fire in the living room, intent on our father as he read to us, the curtains shutting out the black night.

Elisabeth Cowey *Age 13*

A father is a person who you love very much. He is never tired of hearing your jokes.

Eduardo Vivo *Age 8*

My house is lonely when my father is at work.

Clara Ortega *Age 8*

A father is for staying home to be with his son.

Robert McConchie *Age 12*

Dalton Exley

Kung fu dads

My dad holds me by the middle, and says one, two, three. He pretends that he is going to throw me out of the window, but he realy throws me on to my bed.

Nicola Jane Hickson *Age 8*

My dad is the kind of person that does Kung Fu on me and pulls me out of bed with a Kratie chop. Every weekend he gets my big brother to teach me how to kick my dad back. **Andrew Pinder** *Age 10*

Fathers are people that will fight with you but not hurt you.

Christine Johnston *Age 11*

Harold *Age 9*

Ferhan Kurtulmus Age 9

Dad's know what it is like
to be a kid and they know what
we will be up to like kicking
gates and knocking on doors.
Dave Age 14

My dad is very good at
Monopoly. He makes the
rules up as he goes along.
Fraser Age 11

When his team win a game
he leaps up in the air,
screeching "Yippee!" or
"Yahooh!" or "Yahay!".
Sophia Davies Age 11

My dad is a big
kid because he
always wants to
read my comics.
Carl Age 8

Witney King

Just a big kid?

When I get my train set out, my dad takes over the controls, and I have to work the switches.
But my dad does have some good points, he lets me take over the controls sometimes about 5 minutes before bed time.

Nigel *Age 10*

David Fraser

Fun and games

My daddy lays on the floor and me and my sister get on him. We pretend he is a donkey.

Susan Lamb Age 5

My father does sports with me even though I get hit by a softball cant reach a basket in basketball and kick balls into the woods in football. I still think it fun.

Andrew Age 8

One of my dad's main pleasures is his golf. He plays in a local team all through the summer. He has the fanciest miss I've ever seen.

David

In the snow dads always pull you along on the sled, and they put up a good snowball fight. If you go out with your dad you can guarantee that you have a good time. Dads always seem to make things fun.

K. Abele

A dad is someone who on the only day he doesn't work takes you swimming.

Elisabeth Fenton Age 12

He helps me ride a bike

Jane Hutchinson Age 7

Father can be a playful fellow.
He'll tell the little children in the
house a joke or two to make
them jolly, to make them
happy, merry children
instead of miserable
grumpy ones.
That's what I like.

Jemima Age 7

Andrew Green

Saturday morning

The thing I like about my dad is he is very cuddly and soft especially on Saturday morning. I always creep in and snuggle up to him.

Suzanne Pinder

On Saturday morning my mother is marvellous. Out of bed she jumps (well, not exactly jumps) but she gets out of bed and down to the kitchen she goes tiptoeing, where she begins her wonders, eggs and tomatoes and beans (on special days) toast and a great cup of coffee for breakfast nothing burned (usually). Meanwhile Daddy is still fast asleep, but as usual his bliss is ended by the four of us jumping on his bed waiting for one of his fantastic stories. I find that Daddy's stories are marvellous, they are exciting, frightening, amusing but above all imaginative. He is very good at those stories (Daddy made) but he always stops when there is a slight hint of breakfast, I wonder why? Daddy (I suppose) is patient, strong-hearted and above all kind. He protects all of us like a shepherd guarding his sheep (he even bleats, that is snores). I don't know where I'd be if my dearest mother and father weren't by my side.

Belinda Scarborough *Age 12*

My dad reminds me of an oak tree. He's big, solid, old, untidy and absolutely grand.

David

Luengo

Habits

I found out about Santa Claus when Dad dropped all our toys on the wooden floor outside my bedroom and from then on I knew why my mother always put beer out for Santa, not milk.

Andrew Simpson

Jeremy Solomon *Age 8*

Thomas Hudson Age 8

My daddy is funy He has false teeth and wen
He gos to Bed He puts them under the Bed and
wen my mommy gos to Bed my daddy false teeth
Bits my mommy and she jumps out of the Bed.

Mary Age 7

My daddy has naughty habbits they are, Daddy
says that Mommy has got is Keys but Mommy
says she hasn't and Daddy says she has so
Mommy says Look in your pocket so Daddy looks
in his pocket and all that time he had them in his
pocket.

Tracey Age 8

Kids on dads. . .

One day my dad got married to a lady, her name was Elaine. Then they went on a honeymoon and they had a baby boy. His name is Brian but they had another baby, when they came home. It was a little baby girl. Its name was Sherry. After a couple of weeks my mother had me and she named me Rebecca.

Rebecca

Tina Vowles Age

A dad is a male mate to a woman. They buy a new house. And then they babysit their new children.

Erika Age

My mother likes to have babies, but my father doesn't like to have babies.

Paul Age

New dads always take on a smug self-satisfied expression of haven't-we-done-well, and they love having their little Achievement admired. But once the little achievement learns how to a) bawl incessantly b) ask for money and pull tablecloths from tables – "like the man did on TV" – their faces change to an expression of why-did-we-bother.

Lorraine Phelps

Neil King *Age 9*

I think a father is a human being who watches you grow up into his little girl. Then he has something to brag about to his friends.

Debbie *Age 11*

Holding forth. . .

Dads of today seem to spend most of their waking moments telling their unfortunate offspring how much harder life was in their day and yet never waste a moment in saying what a state the country's in and start reminiscing about the Good Old Days.

Julia

"Waste Not, Want Not" is a phrase that continually escapes from Dad's lips, seconded only by "When-I-was-your-age-I-didn't-have-as-much-as-you-do-now" and "Kids!".

Lorraine

Every person needs a dad
But sometimes they are a bore,
When Dad is saying
What he did in the war.

Geraint *Age 12*

Fathers are always right, and even if they're not right, they're never actually wrong.

Catherine *Age 12*

Money

Dads are like moving banks.

John *Age 11*

I don't get much money I think there should be a law that you double your child's money or else you have to go to jail.

Debbie

My father is a sport fanatic, especially for football. In the evening if his team has lost he is gloomy and down-hearted. When it wins he's glowing with excitement; now is the time to ask for that extra money.

Fiona *Age 13*

My dad is a cop but even so my dad still sneaks money out of my mom's purse.

Mandy

When Dad comes home from work he likes me to give him a big hug and I do, especially on pay days.

Kristin

Lincoln Age 10

Every week
Dad gives me
too little money.
How am I supposed to
live with
inflation?

Kelly

Growing pains

My dad is always shouting at me and not my little sisster wich ido-not think is fair. My little sisster dosent seem to think what i think she seems to think it is fair of course LITTLE SISSTERS are awful.

John *Age 9*

My father at lunch time says *"Stop making that noise"* making more noise than anyone else.

Patricia *Age 9*

Daddies are always on at you. Daddy says "Go to bed at 8 o'Clock" when I don't go 'til 8:15. And insists homework is done properly and is always reminding about being polite. OH PARENTS.

Rebecca *Age 10*

Dads are always looking for things to yell at you for, like to stand up when someone older than you comes in; I think it's just a waste of time.

John *Age 10*

If a father asks his son to bring him the slippers, he will obey right away; but if a son kindly requires his father to do the same, the slippers will be thrown upon his head.

Alberto *Age 14*

Up to Bed. Why?
Get in the Bath. Why?
Because you're dirty
Go and put the milk on!
Supper's ready. What is it?
Come and see. Oh Yum, Yum.
Don't pick.
Can I watch X-Files No!

Duncan *Age 9*

My dad is always on to us
about being rude (as though he
is such an angel.) Yet every day
when we're eating, (especially
when we have guests) he comes
up with rude subjects (which I
won't mention). My dad is
always on to me about swearing.
BUT! I have heard him swear
five times in the last few days.
When he is driving the car, for
some mysterious reason he
keeps on picking his nose. Yet he
is always on to us about these
things. If I told you some of the
things he did when he was a
boy I could go on forever,
so I'd better stop now.

Stephen

Sarah Gammen

A big softy

My dad's kindness changes everything.

Jane Livermore *Age 11*

My Dad is a softy,
he does tell me off sometimes but he makes a
weedy effort.

Sam Mcrory *Age 9*

My daddy is like clay, he is all hard and gritty,
but when we do something like sweep the floor he
goes all soft and smiley.

Gemma *Age 11*

I like my dad because when he tells me off
he says it in a soft deep voice and I don't feel hurt
at all.

Tracy Sims *Age 9*

In the eighteenth century a father was hard on
the outside and inside. By the twenties he was
hard outside but soft inside. Nowadays he is soft
both outside and inside.

Mark

Father means love

A man becomes a father only when his wife gives birth to a child. Till then he is only an ordinary man. When a man becomes a father he becomes the most responsible man on the earth.

Sandeep Sampat *Age 16*

My father is happy but he sometimes sits on his chair looking sad and would not part from us for all the riches in the world.

Judy S. Garcia *Age 9*

When we get a big job we must not forget them because when we were small they did not forget us. When they are old and sick we must not leave then as strangers.

Michael M. Rambert *Age 11*

Euan Leckie *Age 7*

Some dads give them everything except love, some give them nothing but love.

Aysegul Corekci *Age 15*

Always there for me

I love you because you are always there for me and you always love and care for me.

Lisa Weintroub *Age 11*

My dad's lovely he is just for me.

Mandy Tiwana *Age 11*

I wish for you a Rolls Royce car, and a luxury trip to France. I wish for you to be able to go to football matches or golf matches without having to look after me. I wish for you to be happy. I wish for you to have nice clothes and go out to posh Restaurants without costing you an arm and a leg. But most of all I wish you to have a good life without being stressed.

Danielle Green *Age 10*

God keep our fathers as nice as they have always been

Jane Moppel *Age 12*

Suzanne Causer *Age 6*